Questions Literacy Resources

Please Mrs Butler and Heard it in the Playground

Questions Literacy Resources

Please Mrs Butler and Heard it in the Playground

Compiled by Michael and Kate Lockwood

Activities and teachers' notes
based on the poems by Allan Ahlberg

THE *QUESTIONS* PUBLISHING COMPANY LTD
BIRMINGHAM
2001

The Questions Publishing Company Ltd
27 Frederick Street, Birmingham B1 3HH

First published in 2001

ISBN: 1 84190 049 4

Illustrations by Martin Cater
Printed in the UK

Acknowledgements
The poems and illustrations in Part 1 of this book are reproduced by permission of Penguin Books Ltd, 27 Wrights Lane, London W8 5TZ.

'Please Mrs Butler' (p. 10), 'Slow Reader' (p. 13), 'There's a Fish Tank' (pp. 14-15), 'Emma Hackett's Newsbook' (pp.18-19), 'As I was Coming to School' (p. 29), 'Complaint' (p. 32), 'Picking Teams' (p. 35), 'Excuses' (p. 61), 'reading test' (p. 63), 'Only Snow' (pp. 66-67), 'Do a Project' (pp. 76), 'Lost' (pp78-79), 'Scabs' (pp. 91-92) and accompanying illustrations by Fritz Wegner are taken from PLEASE MRS BUTLER by Allan Ahlberg (Kestrel, 1983) Copyright (c) Allan Ahlberg, 1983.

Teacher's Prayer, Registration (p. 11), Sale of Work (p. 15), Bags I (pp. 30-31), Where's Everybody (p. 34), The Boy Without a Name (p. 44), Things I have been Doing Lately (p. 46), Mrs So-and-so (pp. 55-56), The Mad Professor's Daughter (pp. 67-72) and accompanying illustrations by Fritz Wegner are taken from HEARD IT IN THE PLAYGROUND by Allan Ahlberg (Viking, 1989) Copyright (c) Allan Ahlberg, 1989.

Also available from The Questions Publishing Company Ltd:

Questions Literacy Resources

Bill's New Frock
based on the novel by Anne Fine and compiled by Marian Dean

The Story of Tracy Beaker
based on the novel by Jacqueline Wilson and compiled by Liz Ross

Contents

Introduction: how to use this book

Part 1: Poems

Part 2: Activities for the Literacy Hour

Part 3: Activities outside the Literacy Hour

Part 1:
Poems

Please Mrs Butler

Please Mrs Butler
This boy Derek Drew
Keeps copying my work, Miss.
What shall I do?

Go and sit in the hall, dear.
Go and sit in the sink.
Take your books on the roof, my lamb.
Do whatever you think.

Please Mrs Butler
This boy Derek Drew
Keeps taking my rubber, Miss.
What shall I do?

Keep it in your hand, dear.
Hide it up your vest.
Swallow it if you like, my love.
Do what you think best.

Please Mrs Butler
This boy Derek Drew
Keeps calling me rude names, Miss.
What shall I do?

Lock yourself in the cupboard, dear.
Run away to sea.
Do whatever you can, my flower.
But *don't ask me!*

Where's Everybody?

In the cloakroom
Wet coats
Quietly steaming.

In the office
Dinner-money
Piled in pounds.

In the head's room
Half a cup
Of cooling tea.

In the corridor
Cupboards
But no crowds.

In the hall
Abandoned
Apparatus.

In the classrooms
Unread books
And unpushed pencils.

In the infants
Lonely hamster
Wendy house to let;

Deserted Plasticine
Still waters
Silent sand.

In the meantime
In the playground...
A fire-drill.

Things I Have Been Doing Lately

Things I have been doing lately:
Pretending to go mad
Eating my own cheeks from the inside
Growing taller
Keeping a secret
Keeping a worm in a jar
Keeping a good dream going
Picking a scab on my elbow
Rolling the cat up in a rug
Blowing bubbles in my spit
Making myself dizzy
Holding my breath
Pressing my eyeballs so that I become temporarily blind
Being very nearly ten
Practising my signature ...

Saving the best till last.

Slow Reader

I – am – in – the – slow
read – ers – group – my –broth
er – is – in – the – foot
ball – team – my – sis – ter
is – a – ser – ver – my
lit – tle – broth – er – was
a – wise – man – in – the
in – fants – christ – mas – play
I – am – in – the – slow
read – ers – group – that – is
all – I – am – in – I
hate – it.

reading test

tree	little	milk	egg	book
read	ing	test	I	took
school	sit	frog	playing	bun
it	was	not	much	fun
flower	road	clock	train	light
still	I	got	it	right
picture	think	summer	peo . . .	
			popple . . .	
			peep . . .	
			pe . . .	
			p . . . well, nearly.	

Bags I

Bags I the dummy
Bags I the cot
Bags I the rubber duck
The other baby's got.

Bags I the cricket ball
Wickets and bat
Bags I the hamster
Bags I the cat.

Bags I the pop records
Hear the music throb
Bags I the A levels
Bags I the job.

Bags I the sweetheart
Lovers for life
Bags I the husband
Bags I the wife.

Bags I the savings
The mortgage and then
Bags I the baby –
Here we go again!

Bags I not the glasses
The nearly bald head
Bags under eyes
And the middle-aged spread.

Bags I the memories
How it all began
Bags I the grandpa
Bags I the gran.

Bags I the hearing-aid
Bags I the stick
Bags I the ending
Quiet and quick.

Goodbye world!
Goodbye me!
Bags I the coffin
RIP.

Registration

Emma Hackett?
Here, Miss!
Billy McBone?
Here, Miss!
Derek Drew?
Here, Miss!
Margaret Thatcher?*
Still here, Miss!

Long John Silver?
Buccaneer, Miss!
Al Capone?
Racketeer, Miss!
Isambard Kingdom Brunel?
Engineer, Miss!
Davy Crockett?
Wild frontier, Miss!
Frank Bruno?
Cauliflower ear, Miss!

The White rabbit?
Late, Miss!
Billy the Kid?
Infants, Miss!
Simple Simon?
Here, Sir!
Father Christmas?
Present (for you), Miss!
Count Dracula?
1, 2, 3, 4, Miss!
Necks door, Miss!
Dentist's!

The Invisible Man?
Nowhere, Miss!
Almighty God?
Everywhere, Miss!
Tarzan?
Aaaaaaaaaah! Miss.
Sleeping Beauty?
Zzz, Miss.

* Long-serving British prime minister (1979–90)

Emma Hackett's Newsbook

Last night my mum
Got really mad
And threw a jam tart
At my dad.
Dad lost his temper
Then with mother,
Threw one at her
And hit my brother.
My brother thought
It was my sister
Threw two at her
But somehow missed her.
My sister,
She is only three,
Hurled four at him
And one at me!

I said I wouldn't
Stand for that,
Aimed one at her
And hit the cat.
The cat jumped up
Like he'd been shot,
And landed
In the baby's cot.
The baby –
Quietly sucking his thumb –
Then started howling
For my mum.
At which my mum
Got *really* mad,
And threw a Swiss roll
At my dad.

Do a Project

Do a project on dinosaurs.
Do a project on sport.
Do a project on the Empire State Building,
The Eiffel Tower,
The Blackpool Tower,
The top of a bus.

Ride a project on horses.
Suck a project on sweets.
Play a project on the piano.
Chop a project on trees
Down.

Write a project on paper,
A plaster cast,
The back of an envelope,
The head of a pin.

Write a project on the Great Wall of China,
Hadrian's Wall,
The playground wall,
Mrs Wall.

Do a project in pencil,
In ink,
In half an hour,
In bed,
Instead
Of something else,
In verse,
Or worse;
Do a project in playtime.

Do a project on your hands and knees,
Your head,
With one arm tied behind you.

Do a project wearing handcuffs,
In a steel coffin,
Eighty feet down
At the bottom of the Hudson River
(Which ideally should be frozen over),
On Houdini.

Forget a project on Memory;
And refuse one on Obedience.

Excuses

I've writ on the wrong page, Miss.
My pencil went all blunt.
My book was upside-down, Miss.
My book was back to front.

My margin's gone all crooked, Miss.
I've smudged mine with my scarf.
I've rubbed a hole in the paper, Miss.
My ruler's broke in half.

My work's blew out the window, Miss.
My work's fell in the bin.
The leg's dropped off my chair, Miss.
The ceiling's coming in.

I've ate a poison apple, Miss.
I've held a poison pen!
I think I'm being *kidnapped*, Miss!
So . . . can we start again?

As I was Coming to School

As I was coming to school, Sir,
To learn my ABC,
I was picked up and put in a sack, Sir,
And carried off on his back, Sir,
By a Russian who took me to sea.

So I had to swim all the way back, Sir,
And I still had my legs in the sack, Sir,
And the waves they were forty foot high, Sir,
Which is really the reason why, Sir –
I would not tell a lie, Sir –
I'm late for school today.

Is it all right to go out to play?

Complaint

The teachers all sit in the staffroom.
The teachers all drink tea.
The teachers all smoke cigarettes
As cosy as can be.

We have to go out at playtime
Unless we bring a note
Or it's tipping down with rain
Or we haven't got a coat.

We have to go out at playtime
Whether we like it or not.
And freeze to death if it's freezing
And boil to death if it's hot.

The teachers can sit in the staffroom
And have a cosy chat.
We have to go out at playtime;
Where's the fairness in that?

Picking Teams

When we pick teams in the playground,
Whatever the game might be,
There's always somebody left till last
And usually it's me.

I stand there looking hopeful
And tapping myself on the chest,
But the captains pick the others first,
Starting, of course, with the best.

Maybe if teams were sometimes picked
Starting with the worst,
Once in his life a boy like me
Could end up being first!

The Boy Without a Name

I remember him clearly
And it was thirty years ago or more:
A boy without a name.

A friendless, silent boy,
His face blotched red and flaking raw,
His expression, infinitely sad.

Some kind of eczema
It was, I now suppose,
The rusty iron mask he wore.

But in those days we confidently swore
It was from playing near dustbins
And handling broken eggshells.

His hands, of course, and knees
Were similarly scabbed and cracked and dry.
The rest of him we never saw.

They said it wasn't catching; still, we knew
And strained away from him along the corridor,
Sharing a ruler only under protest.

I remember the others: Brian Evans,
Trevor Darby, Dorothy Cutler.
And the teachers: Mrs Palmer, Mr Waugh.

I remember Albert, who collected buttons,
And Amos, frothing his milk up with a straw.
But *his* name, no, for it was never used.

I need a time-machine.
I must get back to nineteen fifty-four
And play with him, or talk, at least.

For now I often wake to see
His ordinary, haunting face, his flaw.
I hope his mother loved him.

Oh, children, don't be crueller than you need.
The faces that you spit on or ignore
Will get you in the end.

Only Snow

Outside, the sky was almost brown.
The clouds were hanging low.
Then all of a sudden it happened:
The air was full of snow.

The children rushed to the windows.
The teacher let them go,
Though she teased them for their foolishness.
After all, it was only snow.

It was only snow that was falling,
Only out of the sky,
Only onto the turning earth
Before the blink of an eye.

What else could it do from up there,
But fall in the usual way?
It was only *weather*, really.
What else could you say?

The teacher sat at her desk
Putting ticks in a little row,
While the children stared through steamy glass
At the only snow.

The Mad Professor's Daughter

She came into the classroom
In a dress as black as night
And her eyes were as green as grass
And her face was paper-white.
She was tall and quite unsmiling,
Though her manner was polite.

Yes, her manner was polite
As she stood with Mrs Porter
And you never would have guessed
She was the Mad Professor's daughter.

'A new girl,' said the teacher.
'Her name is Margaret Bell.
She's just arrived this morning.
She's not been very well.'
And we stared into those grass-green eyes
And sank beneath their spell.

Yes, we sank beneath their spell
Like swimmers under water
And found ourselves in thrall
To the Mad Professor's daughter.

The sky outside was overcast;
Rain hung in the air
And splattered on the window panes
As we sat waiting there.
Our fate, we knew, was settled,
Yet we hardly seemed to care.

Yes, we hardly seemed to care,
As the clock ticked past the quarter,
That we had lost our lives
To the Mad Professor's daughter.

We did our sums in a sort of trance,
'Played' at half-past ten,
Sang songs in the hall for half an hour,
Ate lunch and played again.
And all the while, like a constant ache,
We wondered 'Where?' and 'When?'

Yes, where and when and how and why,
And what ill luck had brought her?
And whether we might yet deny
The Mad Professor's daughter.

She made no move at two o'clock.
She made no move at three.
A wisp of hope rose in our hearts
And thoughts of 'mum' and 'tea'.
And then she spoke the fatal words,
Just four: 'Come home with me!'

She spoke the words 'Come home with me'
The way her father taught her;
Her green eyes fixed unblinkingly,
The Mad Professor's daughter.

And now an extra sense of dread
Seeped into every soul;
The hamster cowered in its cage,
The fish flinched in its bowl.
We put our chairs up on the desks
And heard the thunder roll.

Yes, we heard the thunder roll
As we turned from Mrs Porter
And set off through the town
With the Mad Professor's daughter.

Her silent lips were red as blood.
Her step was firm (alas!)
And the people on the street
Stood aside to let us pass.
Though this piper played no tune,
She had enthralled a whole class.

A whole class, like sheep we were,
Like lambs to the slaughter,
With PE bags and such
Behind the Mad Professor's daughter.

The rain beat down upon our heads.
The wind was warm and wild.
Wet trees blew all around us,
As up a drive we filed.
Then a mad face at a window
Stared out at us – and smiled.

Yes, a mad face at a window
That streamed with running water,
While lightning lit the sky above
The Mad Professor's daughter.

And now the end has almost come;
We wait here in despair
With chains upon our arms and legs
And cobwebs in our hair.
And hear her voice outside the door,
His foot upon the stair.

Yes, his foot upon the stair:
'Oh, save us, Mrs Porter!'
Don't leave us to the father of
The Mad Professor's daughter.

A final word – a warning:
Please heed this tale I tell.
If you should meet a quiet girl
Whose name is Margaret Bell,
Don't look into her grass-green eyes
Or you'll be lost as well.

Yes, you'd be lost as well,
However hard you fought her,
And curse until the day you died
The Mad Professor's daughter.

Scabs

The scab on Jean's knee
Is geographical.
Bexhill-on-Sea:
Tripped up on school trip.

The scab on Henry's knee
Is historical.
Oldest scab in Class Three:
Second year sack race.

The scab on Paul's knee
Is pugilistical.
Fighting Clive Key:
He got a cut lip.

The scab on Sally's knee
Is psychological.
Hurts if she does PE:
Painless at playtime.

The scab on Brian's knee
Is bibliographical.
Fooling around in library:
Banged into bookcase.

The scabs on the twins' knees
Are identical.
Likewise the remedies:
Hankies and spit.

The scab on Eric's knee
Is economical.
£2.50:
Second-hand skates.

The scab on Debby's knee
Is diabolical.
Nothing to see:
Hurts like the devil.

psychological

geographical

historical

Teacher's Prayer

Let the children in our care
Clean their shoes and comb their hair;
Come to school on time – and neat
Blow their noses, wipe their feet.
Let them, Lord, **not** eat in class
Or rush into the hall en masse.
Let them show some self-control;
Let them slow down; let them **stroll**!

Let the children in our charge
Not be violent or large;
Not be sick on the school-trip bus,
Not be cleverer than **us**;
Not be unwashed, loud or mad,
(with a six-foot mother or a seven-foot dad).
Let them, please, say 'drew' not 'drawed';
Let them know the **answers**, Lord!

Lost

Dear Mrs Butler, this is just a note
About our Raymond's coat
Which he came home without last night,
So I thought I'd better write.

He was minus his scarf as well, I regret
To say; and his grandma is most upset
As she knitted it and it's pure
Wool. You'll appreciate her feelings, I'm sure.

Also, his swimming towel has gone
Out of his PE bag, he says, and one
Of his socks, too – it's purplish and green
With a darn in the heel. His sister Jean

Has a pair very similar. And while
I remember, is there news yet of those fairisle
Gloves which Raymond lost that time
After the visit to the pantomime?

Well, I think that's all. I will close now,
Best wishes, yours sincerely, Maureen Howe
(Mrs). P.S. I did once write before
About his father's hat that Raymond wore

In the school play and later could not find,
But got no reply. Still, never mind,
Raymond tells me now he might have lost the note,
Or left it in the pocket of his coat.

Sale of Work

Who wants to buy:
Twenty sums, half right,
Two tracings of Francis Drake,
A nearly finished project on dogs
And a page of best handwriting?

Price reduced for quick sale:
Junk model of the Taj Mahal.
Delivery can be arranged.

What am I bid
For this fine old infant's newsbook
Complete with teacher's comments?

Hurry, hurry, hurry!
Brand-new paintings going cheap –
Still wet!

Mrs So-and-so

In the classroom
Sits a teacher,
Who she is we do not know.
Our own teacher's
Feeling poorly,
We've got Mrs So-and-so.

Our own teacher's
Firm but friendly,
Lets us play out in the snow.
Lets us dawdle
In the cloakroom,
Not like Mrs So-and-so.

Stop that pushing!
Stop that shoving!
Line up quietly in a row.
Somehow life
Is not the same with
Bossy Mrs So-and-so.

Our own teacher's
Kind and clever –
Not a lot she doesn't know.
Where's the pencils?
What's your name, dear?
Says this Mrs So-and-so.

Now at last
Our teacher's better
And it's time for *her* to go.
Funny thing is
Somehow we've got ...
Used to Mrs So-and-so.

There's a Fish Tank

There's a fish tank
In our class
With no fish in it;
A guinea-pig cage
With no guinea-pig in it;
A formicarium
With no ants in it;
And according to Miss Hodge
Some of our heads
Are empty too.

There's a stock-cupboard
With no stock,
Flowerpots without flowers,
Plimsolls without owners,
And me without a friend
For a week
While he goes on holiday.

There's a girl
With no front teeth,
And a boy with hardly any hair
Having had it cut.
There are sums without answers,
Paintings unfinished,
And projects with no hope
Of ever coming to an end.
According to Miss Hodge
The only thing that's brim-full
In our class
Is the waste-paper basket.

Part 2:
Activities for the Literacy Hour

Activities for the Literacy Hour

Please Mrs Butler

Year 3, Term 1

Text level reading

Read aloud and enjoy the title poem *Please Mrs Butler*. Ask who is speaking in the first, third and fifth stanzas of the poem. Which words make us assume it's a girl (e.g. *dear, lamb, love, flower*)? What ideas about girls' and boys' behaviour are suggested in the poem and do the class agree with these? Ask the children what they think of Mrs Butler's replies in stanzas two, four and six. Are they what Mrs Butler says or just what she thinks? Discuss the situation in the poem and ask the children about their own experiences of 'telling the teacher'. Perform the poem with two readers, or two groups, taking the child and teacher roles. Talk about the use of rhyme, rhythm, repetition and italics for emphasis in the poem, and review and modify the performance in the light of this. (Text level 1: *read aloud and recite poems, comparing different views of the same subject . . .* Text level 8: *to express their views about a story or poem . . .*)

Text level writing

Tell the children they are going to write some more stanzas for the poem. First ask them to brainstorm ideas for more things a teacher could say in the poem, and for words and phrases she or he might use. Write the suggestions on a large sheet of paper that all the children can see. The children can then use the writing frame on PCM 1 to write their new stanzas. The activity can be differentiated for able writers by not using the frame, and for less able, by only asking for one or two new stanzas. Children could also work in pairs or small groups to complete PCM 1. (Text level 12: *collect suitable words and phrases, in order to write poems . . .*)

Sentence level reading

Focus on the way the poem is structured through different kinds of sentences: statements (e.g. lines 1-3), questions (e.g. line 4) and replies in the form of orders or commands (e.g. lines 5-8). Ask how we can tell the difference between a statement (tells you something), a question (asks something) and a command (tells you to do something). Discuss the use of question marks in punctuation. Talk about the different word order in commands, since verbs usually come first. Demonstrate this by getting the children to give you the first word of all the teacher's replies, except the last line: *go, go, take, do, keep, hide, swallow, do, lock, run, do* (all verbs). (Sentence level 3 : *the function of verbs in sentences through noticing that sentences cannot make sense without them.*)

Ask what kind of sentence the last line is. How is it punctuated? This is an exclamation (tells you about someone's feelings). Why is it appropriate to have this at the end of the poem? (Sentence level 6: *to secure knowledge of question marks and exclamation marks in reading . . .*)

PCM 1
Please Mrs Butler

Write some more replies for the teacher in the poem.
Make up a name for the teacher and decide whether the child is a boy or girl.

Please Mrs/Mr _____
This boy Derek Drew
Keeps pulling funny faces, Miss.
What shall I do?

_____ , dear.

_____
_____ , my treasure.

_____ .

Please Mrs/Mr _____
This boy Derek Drew
Keeps kicking me under the table, Miss.
What shall I do?

_____ , dear.

_____
_____ , my sweetheart.

_____ .

Please Mrs/Mr _____
This boy Derek Drew
Keeps poking me with his pencil, Miss.
What shall I do?

_____ , dear.

_____
_____ , my poppet.

But *don't ask me*!

Activities for the Literacy Hour

Where's Everybody?
Year 3, Term 1

Text level reading

Read aloud and enjoy *Where's Everybody?*, pausing before the final stanza to see whether the class can guess what's happened in the poem. Talk about how the poem is written: it's as if someone were walking round the empty school, going from room to room, observing what's been left behind, taking a snapshot of each place. The poem works by picking out small details for each room to give the feeling of a place that's been abandoned: the writer has used careful observation and different senses to do this. Ask the children to pick out a word or phrase in each stanza which they think is well chosen to describe the scene and create the atmosphere of the empty school. For example:

Wet	*Quietly steaming*
Piled	*Cooling*
Abandoned	*Unread*
Unpushed	*Lonely*
Deserted	*Still*
Silent	

Discuss these words and phrases. Which are the most effective and powerful ones? Can the class think of any alternative words and phrases which could be used instead? Try these synonyms out in the poem and discuss their impact.

(Text level 6: . . . *to discuss choice of words and phrases that describe and create impact, e.g. adjectives, powerful and expressive verbs.*)

Text level writing

Tell the children they are going to write their own versions of the poem and will need to use their powers of imagination and observation, using all the senses they can. Tell the children to go through the different senses in their descriptions of the deserted school, asking themselves for each place:

- What would it look like?
- What would it sound like?
- What would it smell like?
- How would it feel?

Use the framework in PCM 2 and go through each stanza, giving children time to think individually and then share ideas in pairs before asking for possible contributions to the class poem. Stress the need for expressive verbs and, especially, powerful adjectives. Children can use PCM 2 or their own frameworks, according to ability, to write their own individual or collaborative poems during the group time (Text level 12: *to collect suitable words and phrases, in order to write poems and short descriptions . . .*)

PCM 2
Where's everybody?

Write some more descriptions of the empty school.
What would it look like? Sound like? Feel like? Smell like?
Use some expressive verbs and powerful adjectives.

In the cloakroom

_____

_____

In the office

_____

_____

In the head's room

_____

_____

In the corridor

_____

_____

In the hall

_____

_____

In the classrooms

_____

_____

In the infants

_____

_____

In the meantime
In the playground...
A fire-drill.

Activities for the Literacy Hour

Things I Have Been Doing Lately
Year 3, Term 1

Text level writing

Read and enjoy *Things I Have Been Doing Lately*. Discuss the kind of things the speaker mentions in the poem; how they range from things which happen to everybody (*Growing taller*) to things which many children do (*Practising my signature)* to unusual individual things (*Eating my own cheeks from the inside*). Ask which of these things the children have been doing! Ask the children for similar examples in all three categories of 'Things We've Been Doing Lately'. Write up some of these ideas into a class poem or simple list. This could be made into a class display, with a line from each child presented as a speech or thought bubble. This would be particularly suitable for a display after the summer holiday or half-term break. (Text level 12: *to collect suitable words and phrases, in order to write poems and short descriptions . . .)*

Word level reading

Read *Things I Have Been Doing Lately*, first asking the children to spot what all the lines in the poem, apart from the first line, have in common (they all begin with an –*ing* verb). Go through the poem and make a list of the verb stems with the –*ing* endings taken off. Ask which three of these verbs are the odd ones out and why (*make, practise* and *save* because they drop the final e when they take the –*ing* ending). Ask the children to suggest some other verbs ending in e and to give the –*ing* forms of them (e.g. care, have, move, take etc). Can the class think of any new lines for the poem beginning with one of these verbs? (e.g. Caring for my hamster/ Having a good time/Moving all my books into order of height/Taking the bobbles off my jumper etc). (Word level 8: *how the spellings of verbs alter when –ing is added.*)

Sentence level reading

Talk about 'Things We Used To Do'. Ask the children for things they did when they were little. Encourage them to talk in the past tense, e.g.

- ate mashed banana
- drank from a bottle
- splashed in the paddling pool

Write a list of the verbs used in the poem, then next to each verb write the past tense, e.g.

pretending	pretended
eating	ate
growing	grew
keeping	kept
picking	picked
rolling	rolled etc.

Talk about verbs that follow the regular pattern (–ed ending) and irregular verbs. Reinforce this with PCM 3. (Sentence level 4: *to use verb tenses with increasing accuracy in speaking and writing . . .)*

PCM 3
Things I used to do

Complete the lines by putting the verbs in the past tense. The first one has been done for you.

Things I used to do:

Pretended I was a pop singer   (pretend)

_____ ice cream with tomato ketchup   (eat)

_____ in a high chair   (sit)

_____ a three wheeled tricycle   (ride)

_____ down the stairs   (fall)

_____ a lot   (cry)

Now make up some more lines of your own.

_____

_____

_____

_____

_____

_____

_____

But I've grown up a lot since then.

Activities for the Literacy Hour

Slow Reader

Year 3, Term 1

Text level reading

Read aloud and enjoy *Slow Reader*. Ask why it is set out on the page the way it is (i.e. using dashes to break up words and sentences to create the rhythm of a hesitant reader). Does the poem use rhyme, and if not why not? (to make the reading sound more monotonous) Discuss the feelings of the child who is in the 'slow readers' group' in the poem. Why does the speaker 'hate' being in this group? Ask the children to talk about similar experiences they have had where they have had to do things or belong to groupings they hated, at school or outside school. (Text level 6: *to read aloud and recite poems, comparing different views of the same subject…*; Text level 7: *to distinguish between rhyming and non-rhyming poetry and comment on the impact of layout.*)

Text level writing

Slow Reader could be used as a model for adaptation. For example, children could write about being in the 'slow maths group' or the 'slow science group'. They could change the poem to reflect the speaker's progress into the 'improving readers' group', the 'average readers' group' or the 'fast readers' group'? How would the layout of the poem be changed to reflect this?

More able writers could devise their own reading poems, which through their shape, layout on the page or use of fonts have an apt appearance. Ideas for these might be:

● The fun of reading
● Bookworms
● The library
● My favourite reading place
● Quiet reading

Word processing could be used to alter the shape of a text or for different fonts and font sizes. (Text level 13: *to invent … a range of shape poems, selecting appropriate words and careful presentation.*)

Sentence level reading

Talk about the lack of punctuation. Where should there be full stops and capital letters? Give the children time to change the poem into proper sentences with correct sentence punctuation. The end result will be lots of short sentences but each one will contain a verb. (Sentence level 12: *to demarcate the end of a sentence with a full-stop and the start of a new one with a capital letter.*)

The children can then underline the verb in each sentence. They will need to be aware that *am, is, was* etc. are verbs. This can be illustrated by showing that these words are in a particular tense (present or past) and can be treated like other verbs (they can change tense, *am/was, is/was*). (Sentence level 3: *the function of verbs in sentences through noticing that sentences cannot make sense without them.*)

Word level reading

Clap each syllable in the poem. The children should hear that there are five claps for each line. Which words only have one clap? Which need two claps? The children should be familiar with the concept of syllables so this is an opportunity to revise it. Give them some long words and ask them to read them in the style of the poem. Tell them that it helps all of us, good or not so good at reading, to break longer or unfamiliar words into syllables to help to read or write them. Suitable words to try might be

hippopotamus   (hipp-o-pot-a-mus)
spectacular   (spec-tac-u-lar)
promontory   (pro-mon-tor-y)
articulated   (ar-tic-u-lat-ed)
presentation   (pre-sent-a-tion)
outstandingly   (out-stand-ing-ly)
nationality   (na-tion-a-lit-y)
metamorphosis   (met-a-mor-pho-sis)
experimental   (ex-per-i-ment-al)
congratulations   (con-grat-u-la-tions)
rhododendron   (rho-do-den-dron)

Write the words with gaps between the syllables so that the children can see the individual letter strings. Look for familiar strings, e.g. *or*, *ar*, *tion*. By breaking the words up, it becomes easier to read, and spell, longer words. This can be a very satisfying activity for children who generally struggle with reading. (Word level 4: *to discriminate syllables in reading and spelling*.)

The meanings of some of these words will be unfamiliar. This is an opportunity to extend vocabulary and use a dictionary to find the meanings of words. (Word level 13: *to collect new words ... and log them.* Word level 15: *to have a secure understanding of the purpose and organisation of the dictionary*.)

It is suggested that you follow on from this poem by looking at *reading test*.

Activities for the Literacy Hour

reading test
Year 3, Term 1

Text level reading

This activity follows on from the previous work on *Slow Reader*. It is recommended that the children are familiar with *Slow Reader* in order to be able to compare the two poems.

Read aloud and enjoy *reading test*. Talk about the layout of this poem, which is designed to look like lists of words to read in a test. Ask how we know which way to read it (i.e. the words in the right-hand column all rhyme). How does the rhyme make this poem different from *Slow Reader*? Discuss reading or spelling tests and ask for children's experiences and feelings about them. Ask the children to compare the attitude to reading in the poem (*'it was not much fun'*) with that in *Slow Reader*. Talk about times when reading *is* fun for children, favourite times, places and texts for reading. (Text level 6: *read aloud and recite poems, comparing different views of the same subject...;* Text level 7: *to distinguish between rhyming and non-rhyming poetry and comment on the impact of layout.*)

Text and word level writing

Tell the group they are going to create a shape poem on the subject of reading. The children could begin by creating calligrams: poems where the handwriting or choice of font is appropriate for the subject. Give the group individual words and phrases (e.g. book, ghost story, horror story) and ask them simply to present the words in an appropriate style (e.g. book written as if down the spine of a book).

The group could then move on to creating their own shape poems. PCM 4 could be used to create their own versions of *reading test*. Explain that it will be necessary to end the first line with a word that rhymes with *took*. The children can make their own word bank, e.g.

cook
hook
look
shook
crook

They will need similar lists of words rhyming with *fun* and *right*. This is a good opportunity to reinforce the letter strings *–ook* and *–ight*. (Text level 13: *to invent calligrams and a range of shape poems ... Word level 6: to use independent spelling strategies, including... spelling by analogy with other known words, e.g. light, fright.*)

PCM 4

Shape poem

Put words in the spaces to complete the poem.
Choose words that might be in a real reading test.
Remember to make the words rhyme at the end of each pair of lines.

READING TEST

_____	_____	_____	_____	_____
read	ing	test	I	took

_____	_____	_____	_____	_____
it	was	not	much	fun

_____	_____	_____	_____	_____
still	I	got	it	right

_____

_____

_____

_____ …well, nearly.

Activities for the Literacy Hour

Bags I

Year 3, Term 2

Text level reading

Read aloud and enjoy *Bags I*. Talk about the content of the poem: how it goes from birth through childhood and adolescence to middle age, old age and death. Talk about the form of the poem, the way it uses the rhyming and repetitive structure of a playground chant. Ask the children for other examples of playground chants or choosing dips ('Ip, dip, sky blue'; 'Eeny, meeney, miney, mo' etc.). Talk about where these come from and how they seem to be passed on to generations of different children.

Organise a performance of the poem involving as many children as possible, combining appropriate actions with the words of the poem. For instance, the poem could be performed as a skipping rhyme by a group of children, with other children in the background miming the different ages described in each stanza. Rehearse and modify the performance, possibly using a tape or video recorder for 'drafting' the spoken text. (Text level 4: *to choose and prepare poems for performance, identifying appropriate expression, tone, volume and use of voices and other sounds;* Text level 5: *rehearse and improve performance, taking note of punctuation and meaning.*)

Text level writing

Ask the group to use the repetitive playground-chant structure of *Bags I* to write their own poems. The poems could also be about the different ages of life, or about the different seasons or months of the year, the days of the week, the different subjects of the school curriculum, the different years of primary school, or any other suitable subject. The poems could rhyme as in *Bags I* or be in free verse. PCM 5 gives a simple framework which could be used if appropriate. (Text level 11: *to write new or extended verses for performance based on models of 'performance' and oral poetry read, e.g. rhythms, repetition.*)

Sentence level

Talk about how the poem is written in the first person. Give the children a few moments to think of things that they would include in a similar poem about themselves, e.g. I wish I could have a bedroom of my own. I want to be able to swim without armbands.

Write a few of the children's answers on the board, selecting a variety of verbs, e.g. I wish…, I hope…, I want…, I would like…

Explain that if we were talking about someone else we would have to change the verb slightly. Put the children in pairs. Let them tell each other their own answers. Get the children to report back on what their partner said, e.g. "Sam said he *wishes* he could…."

Emphasise the differences between, e.g. Sam saying "I wish" and his partner saying "he wishes". Rewrite the examples already on the board in the third person and look at how the verbs change. (Sentence level work 10: *to understand the differences between verbs in the first and third person through…experimenting and transforming sentences and noting which words need to be changed.*)

PCM 5
Bags I

Write your own poem based on Allan Ahlberg's.

The poem could be about:

● the different stages of life
● the different seasons
● the months of the year
● the days of the week
● the different subjects of the school timetable
● the different years of primary school

The poem could rhyme or be in free verse.

Bags I the _____

Bags I the _____

Bags I the _____

_____

Bags I the _____

_____

Bags I the _____

Bags I the _____

Bags I the _____

_____

Bags I the _____

Bags I the _____

by _____

Activities for the Literacy Hour

Registration

Year 3, Term 2

Text level reading

Organise a performance of *Registration*, involving as many children as possible. Rehearse and modify the performance, possibly using a tape recorder for 'drafting' the spoken text. Emphasise the use of appropriate intonation to match the punctuation in the poem (question marks and exclamation marks only) and the need for a variety of different voices in the responses of the pupils. (Text level 4: *to choose and prepare poems for performance, identifying appropriate expression, tone, volume and use of voices and other sounds;* Text level 5: *rehearse and improve performance, taking note of punctuation and meaning.*)

Text level writing

Invite the children to suggest other possible names for the register and the responses that might be given. For instance:

- Alan Shearer (Offside, Miss!)
- Snow White (Ate a dodgy apple, Miss!)
- E.T. (Gone home, Miss!)
- Tom Thumb (Down here, Miss!)

Include some of these in an extended performance of *Registration.* Children can then create their own versions of the poem using PCM 6. (Text level 11: *to write new or extended verses for performance based on models of 'performance' and oral poetry read, e.g. rhythms, repetition.*)

Text level reading

Working in pairs, the children can prepare similar performances of other poems such as:

- *Who Knows?* (*PMB* 20-21)
- *Blame* (*PMB* 22)
- *The Challenge* (*PMB* 86-87)

Working in groups of about four, they can prepare performances of:

- *Complaint* (*PMB* 32-33)
- *The Gang* (*PMB* 40-41)
- *Excuses* (*PMB* 61)
- *Do a Project* (*PMB* 76-77)
- *Bags I* (*HP*, 30-31)
- *Parents' Evening* (*HP*, 36-37)

For solo performance:

- *My name is Mrs Brady* (HP 82)
- *Small Quarrel* (PMB 26-27)
- *It is a Puzzle* (PMB 48-49)
- *Scissors* (PMB 56-57)
- *Supply Teacher* (PMB 16-17)

(Text level 4: *to choose and prepare poems for performance, identifying appropriate expression, tone, volume and use of voices and other sounds;* Text level 5: *rehearse and improve performance, taking note of punctuation and meaning.*)

PCM 6
Registration

Start your own version of Allan Ahlberg's poem by putting some children's names into the spaces. Begin with your own name:

_____ ?

Here, Miss!

_____ ?

Here, Miss!

_____ ?

Here, Miss!

Now put in the name of someone you wish wasn't here:

_____ ?

Still here, Miss!

Next put in some appropriate replies for these well-known people. These could be song titles, famous things they have said or to do with what the person does:

The Spice Girls?

_____ , Miss!

David Beckham?

_____ , Miss!

J.K. Rowling?

_____ , Miss!

Finish the poem with some funny replies for these cartoon characters:

Popeye?

_____ , Miss!

Buzz Lightyear?

_____ , Miss!

Bart Simpson?

_____ , Miss!

If you can think of more ideas, write them on the other side of this sheet.

Activities for the Literacy Hour
Emma Hackett's Newsbook
Year 3, Term 3

Text level reading
Organise a performance or reading aloud of *Emma Hackett's Newsbook*. Each of the eight groups of four lines could be read by individuals or groups of children. Then ask the class to recount the chain of events described in the poem, possibly drawing a large diagram on the board to show who threw what at whom. Talk about other comic experiences like these where one thing has led to another, or fights using food. Discuss what helps to make the poem a humorous rather than a serious one, for example the use of short lines with full rhymes, like *mad/dad; mother/brother; sister/missed her*. (Text level 7: *to select, prepare, read aloud and recite by heart poetry that plays with language or entertains; to recognise rhyme, alliteration and other patterns of sound that create effects.*)

Sentence level reading
On an enlarged version of the poem, identify and underline these words used in the opening eight lines: *my, his, her*. Ask why we use words like these and what job they do in sentences. Illustrate this function by reading out a version of the poem's opening without the words:

Last night Emma Hackett's mum
Got really mad
And threw a jam tart
At Emma Hackett's dad.
Dad lost his temper
Then with mother,
Threw one at Emma Hackett's mother
And hit Emma Hackett's brother.

Talk about how words such as *my, his, her* help the writer to avoid repetition of nouns, especially names. Introduce or reinforce the term 'pronoun' as a word that stands *for* a noun ('<u>pro</u>-noun'). Ask for examples of other pronouns we use to stand for people's names (e.g. *mine, hers, they, we,* etc.). Identify all the other pronouns in the rest of the poem and discuss why so many pronouns are used and whether it is clear whom they refer to. Investigate which pronoun is used most frequently and why (*my*).

If appropriate, go on to distinguish possessive from personal pronouns. Ask which pronouns in the poem show something or someone belongs to a person. Underline possessive pronouns in one colour (*my, his*), and personal pronouns in another (*her, him, me, she, I, he*). (Sentence level 2: *to identify pronouns and understand their functions in sentences...*)

Text level writing
Ask the children to plan and then draft another entry for Emma Hackett's newsbook in poem form. It should be humorous like the original one and could be about food being thrown around again or something else. Some of the original rhymes in the poem could be used again (*mad/dad; mother/brother; sister/missed her; three/me; that/cat; thumb/mum*) and the poem could follow the same rhythm.

If the draft is revised and edited into finished form, it could be presented like the page from a school newsbook, or illustrated with small drawings showing the people, food or actions involved, like Fritz Wegner's drawings in the Puffin edition of *Please Mrs Butler*. (Text level 15: *to write poetry that uses sound to create effects, e.g. onomatopoeia, alliteration, distinctive rhythms.*)

Word level reading

Count how many times the word *threw* appears in the poem. (4 times)
Use a thesaurus or ask the children to brainstorm and collect synonyms for *threw*. Suggestions might include:

slung
lobbed
chucked
hurled
tossed
propelled
heaved

Look at alternatives for *said* in the line *I said I wouldn't stand for that.* Suggestions might include:

commented
complained
stated.

Compare this to the different mood created by the word *howling* and its synonyms (shouting, crying, screaming etc.). Talk about other synonyms for *said* and give the children time to compile their own list. These could be displayed on word ladders starting with the quietest at the bottom and leading to the noisiest at the top, e.g.

Children will enjoy the open-ended challenge of creating taller ladders. Ladders can also be created for different types of verbs, e.g. words ranging from *suggested* to *demanded*, or from *asked* to *pleaded*. (Word level 13: *to collect synonyms that will be useful in writing dialogue...*)

There are other words in the poem that could also be replaced by synonyms. Give the children copies of PCM 7 and let them write their own alterations to the original poem. The children need to be aware that a synonym must have a similar meaning to the original so it is not acceptable, for example, to change *quietly* into *noisily*.

After completing PCM 7 the children can compare their solutions with each other.

PCM 7

Emma Hackett's Newsbook

Write synonyms for the original words from the poem, to make up your own version.
You can use a thesaurus for ideas.

Last night my _____*Mother*_____ (mum)

Got _____ (really) mad

And _____ (threw) a jam tart

At my dad.

Dad lost his _____ (temper)

_____ (Then) with mother

_____ (Threw) one at her

And _____ (hit) my brother.

My brother _____ (thought)

It was my sister,

_____ (Threw) two at her

But somehow missed her.

My sister,

She is only three,

_____ (Hurled) four at him

And one at me!

I _____ (said) I wouldn't

_____ (Stand) for that

_____ (Aimed) one at her

And _____ (hit) the cat.

The cat _____ (jumped) up

Like he'd been shot,

And _____ (landed)

In the baby's cot.

The baby –

_____ (Quietly) sucking his thumb –

Then started _____ (howling)

For my mum.

At which my mum

Got _____ (really) mad,

And _____ (threw) a Swiss roll

At my dad.

Activities for the Literacy Hour

Do a Project
Year 3, Term 3

Text level reading and writing
Read aloud and enjoy *Do a Project* with the children. Talk about the humour in the poem and the play on the words 'Do a project on/in…' What subjects are mentioned for projects (e.g. dinosaurs, sport)? What ways of doing the projects are mentioned (e.g. on paper, in pencil)? Talk about how the poem starts off with serious projects and ways of writing them and then goes on to list funny ones. Ask for examples of other funny projects or ways of doing them and list these on the board or a large sheet of paper.

Use PCM 8 as a framework either for a collaborative group poem or for individual poems. (Text level 7: *to select, prepare, read aloud and recite by heart poetry that plays with language or entertains…*)

Word level reading
Talk about homonyms that have the same spellings but more than one meaning. How many homonyms can the children find in the poem? (*e.g. play, chop*). Concentrate here on homographs and ignore homonyms with the same sound but different spellings (e.g. homophones such as tied/tide). Reinforce homonyms using PCM 9.

Talk about how a dictionary gives multiple definitions of a word by numbering each definition, starting with the most common. Give the children some homonyms to find in the dictionary. The children can write pairs of sentences using each meaning (e.g. The nurse put a plaster on the <u>cut</u>. Scissors can <u>cut</u> paper.) Choose different homonyms according to the ability of each child. You may choose to use the following suggestions.

Give the children time to browse through a dictionary looking for homonyms.

Easy	Medium	Advanced
change	well	transfer
trainer	stamp	spur
sprout	spring	skirt
skip	shoot	bail
faint	ring	cycle
duck	jam	handle

Choose different dictionaries according to ability. When they have made a list of homonyms, collect up the dictionaries and allow the children time to either write the homonyms in pairs of sentences or give verbal explanations of the meanings of each word.

A lot of jokes are based on homonyms. *(Why is an old car like a baby? They both have a rattle wherever they go. What do you get if you cross a sheep with a kangaroo? A woolly jumper.)* The children will have fun collecting their own jokes or making up jokes based on homonyms. Present the collection of jokes as a class anthology. The work could be written in best handwriting or word-processed on a computer. (Word level 14: *to explore homonyms which have the same spelling but multiple meanings…*)

PCM 8
Do a project

Write your own poem based on Allan Ahlberg's *Do a Project*.
Think about other funny school projects.
Think about funny ways of doing them.

Do a project on the Romans.

Do a project on _____ .

Do a project on the _____ ,

The _____ ,

The _____ ,

The computer.

Drive a project on _____ .

_____ a project on food.

Read a project on _____ .

_____ a project on television.

Write a project on paper,

On _____ ,

On _____ ,

On _____ .

Do a project in pencil,

In _____ ,

In _____ ,

In _____ ,

Instead

of something else.

PCM 9
Pairs of homonyms

Complete these sentences.
You need to find one homonym for each pair of sentences. All the answers are in the poem *Do a Project.*

1. We went to the theatre to see a _____
I am learning to _____ the recorder.

2. When I fell down, Mum put a _____ on my knee.
The brick wall was covered in _____.

3. The spinning _____ whizzed round and round.
The climber looked at the view from the _____ of the mountain.

4. The cook served lamb _____ and mint sauce.
The woodcutter liked to _____ down trees.

5. If you borrow a pencil you must remember to give it _____ .
The man broke his _____ when he fell out of the tree.

6. The crown was placed carefully on the Queen's _____ .
The teacher stood at the _____ of the line.

7. The twins each sleep in a bunk _____ .
The flower _____ was full of weeds.

Think of two meanings for each of these homonyms.
You can use a dictionary to help you.

match

_____

_____

watch

_____

_____

charge

_____

_____

mouse

_____

_____

Activities for the Literacy Hour

Excuses
Year 4, Term 1

Text level reading
Organise a reading aloud of *Excuses*. Different individuals could read each line or different groups could read each stanza, with everyone joining in on the last line. Talk about the excuses given in the poem and how they become more unbelievable as the poem goes on. Ask for examples of excuses the children have used or heard themselves. You can probably recall some unusual excuses that have been given to you!

Discuss the regular patterns of rhyme and rhythm used throughout. Ask why the poet has used non-standard verb forms such as: *I've writ; My ruler's broke in half; My work's blew out the window; My work's fell in the bin; I've ate.* (These are forms people sometimes use in speech, especially children, so they make the excuses sound more real.)

It is suggested that you follow on from this poem by looking at *As I was Coming to School* and comparing it to *Excuses*. (Text level 7: *compare and contrast poems on similar themes, particularly their form and language, discussing personal responses and preferences.*)

Text and word level writing
Tell the children they are going to write a collaborative *Excuses* poem. Ask them for examples of different excuses they have used either at home or at school when they have been in trouble. List these briefly on the board or a large sheet of paper. Ask the children to select which ones to use in the poem and then revise these words, phrases and clauses by changing, adding or taking out words. Where the excuses are very exaggerated ones, emphasise the choice of effective verbs ('the dog *gobbled* my PE shorts'), but aim to make the poem sound like real speech overall. The poem could be written simply as a list in free verse or it could follow the stanza pattern of *Excuses*, ending the first and third lines with '*Miss*' or '*Sir*' and rhyming the second and fourth lines. A rhyming dictionary could be introduced as a way of finding effective rhyme words in this case. (Text level 14: *to write poems based on real or imagined experience, linked to poems read. List brief phrases and words, experiment by trimming or extending sentences; experiment with powerful and expressive verbs.*)

Sentence level reading
Look at the non-standard verbs in the poem and change them into standard English. Reinforce this with PCM 10. All the verbs used on this PCM are irregular and it provides an opportunity to talk about how not all verbs are written in the past tense by simply adding –*ed*. (Sentence level 1: *to identify errors and suggest alternative constructions.* Sentence level 2: *Revise work on verb tenses...*)

PCM 10

Excuses writ wrong

These excuses have been written in non-standard English.
First underline the words which are in non-standard English.
Then rewrite them in standard English.

1. I've writ on the wrong page.

2. My ruler's broke in half.

3. My work's blew out the window.

4. My work's fell in the bin.

5. I've ate a poison apple.

6. I forgetted what you told me to do.

7. My pencil case zip is sticked.

8. The ink in my pen runned out.

9. My friend told me the wrong page.

10. The fire alarm has goed off.

PCM 10

Activities for the Literacy Hour

As I was Coming to School
Year 4, Term 1

Text level reading
This activity follows on from the previous work on *Excuses*. It is recommended that the children are familiar with *Excuses* in order to be able to compare the two poems.

Read aloud and enjoy *As I was Coming to School*. Ask the children to compare this poem to *Excuses*. What is similar? (e.g. the subject, the use of regular patterns of rhyme and rhythm, the way the poem ends etc.) What is different? (e.g. the poem is spoken by one child only, it uses repetition of 'Sir' instead of 'Miss', it's about one long unbelievable excuse not lots of different ones, it uses more elaborate, storytelling language etc.)

Talk about which poem the children prefer and why, or which parts of each poem they prefer. PCM 11 can be used to structure a comparison between the two poems. (Text level 7: *to compare and contrast poems on similar themes, particularly their form and language, discussing personal responses and preferences.*)

Word level writing
Try finishing some other ridiculous excuses by writing some rhyming couplets:

As I was coming to school, Sir,
I was eaten by a snake, Sir

Get the children to find words that rhyme with snake (ache, bake, break, cake, flake, lake, mistake etc.) by using a rhyming dictionary. Can they use one of these words to complete the excuse?

E.g. Who mistook me for some cake, Sir *or* Then spat me out in the lake, Sir

Can they use a similar method to complete these couplets?

As I was coming to school, Sir,
I fell down a big hole, Sir

As I was coming to school, Sir,
I was pounced on by a cat, Sir

As I was coming to school, Sir,
I was kidnapped by a thing, Sir

Some children could make up their own couplets from scratch.
(Word level 13: *to use a rhyming dictionary, e.g. in composing jingles.*)

PCM 11

Comparing poems

1. What words or phrases did you most enjoy in *Excuses*?

2. What words or phrases did you most enjoy in *As I was Coming to School*?

3. What was similar about the two poems?

4. What was different about the two poems?

5. Which poem did you prefer? _____

Why?

Activities for the Literacy Hour

Complaint

Year 4, Term 1

Text level writing

Share and enjoy *Complaint*, which is about how children view the teachers at playtime. Discuss the grievances that the children in the poem have. Tell the children you want them to write a reply to this poem, which gives the teachers' point of view, looking out from the staffroom window watching the children at playtime. The reply could start off:

The children all play in the playground,
The children all eat snacks.

It could have two stanzas in the middle beginning:

We have to stay in at playtime.

And end with:

We have to stay in at playtime;
Where's the fairness in that?

Ask the children to guess the things that teachers might complain about at playtime (prompting them from your own experience if necessary!) e.g. not being able to run around or play games, not getting any fresh air; having to do playground duty if they do go outside; having to work or have meetings during playtime; having to help children who hurt themselves etc. The teachers' reply could follow the four-stanza structure of the original poem but doesn't have to rhyme second and fourth lines unless desired. (Text level 14: *to write poems based on real or imagined experience, linked to poems read. List brief phrases and words, experiment by trimming or extending sentences; experiment with powerful and expressive verbs.*)

Sentence level reading

Look at the tense of the verbs in the poem. Ask why the poem is written in the present tense. (It is an ongoing complaint that the child who is speaking doesn't feel has ended.)

What verbs can the children find? (*sit, drink, smoke, have to go out, bring,* etc.) Explain that one way to test if a word is a verb is to be able to change its tense.

How can some of these sentences be put into the past tense?
The teachers all sit in the staffroom would become *The teachers all sat in the staffroom.*

Reinforce changing verbs from the present tense into the past tense using PCM 12. (Sentence level 2: *understand that one test of whether a word is a verb is whether or not its tense can be changed.*)

There is another activity based on *Complaint* in Part 3 on p.92.

PCM 12

Past complaints

Rewrite these lines from the poem *Complaint* by putting the underlined verbs into the past tense.

How does the verb change?

1. *Present tense:*   The teachers all <u>sit</u> in the staffroom.
   Past tense: _____
   The verb _____*sit*_____ changes to _____*sat*_____ .

2. *Present tense:*   The teachers all <u>drink</u> tea.
   Past tense: _____
   The verb _____ changes to _____ .

3. *Present tense:*   We <u>have</u> to go out at playtime
   Past tense: _____
   The verb _____ changes to _____ .

4. *Present tense:*   Unless we <u>bring</u> a note
   Past tense: _____
   The verb _____ changes to _____ .

5. *Present tense:*   Or we <u>haven't</u> got a coat.
   Past tense: _____
   The verb _____ changes to _____ .

6. *Present tense:*   Whether we <u>like</u> it or not.
   Past tense: _____
   The verb _____ changes to _____ .

7. *Present tense:*   And <u>freeze</u> to death if it's freezing
   Past tense: _____
   The verb _____ changes to _____ .

8. *Present tense:*   And <u>boil</u> to death if it's hot.
   Past tense: _____
   The verb _____ changes to _____ .

Activities for the Literacy Hour

Picking Teams and *The Boy Without a Name*

Year 4, Term 1

Text level reading

Read and enjoy *Picking Teams.* Discuss the experience of being picked last in situations like the one in the poem. Give children time to remember and then share their own experiences in pairs. Talk about ways in which the situation can be avoided, for example in games and PE lessons. What about the speaker's idea in the poem: *Maybe if teams were sometimes picked/Starting with the worst*? Could it work? Would it be any better?

Read *The Boy without a Name* and compare with *Picking Teams.* Talk about:

- What is meant by *The rusty iron mask he wore*? (dry, red skin)
- What is eczema? (a non-infectious skin condition)
- What do the other children think eczema is and how do they behave to the boy?
- Why can't the poet remember the boy's name?
- How does the poet feel now about the boy?
- What does he mean by: *Will get you in the end*?

Discuss how it feels to be in such a situation. Talk about experiences the children have had or heard about where people have been treated cruelly or ignored because of how they look.

Compare the form and language of the two poems:

- both are in the first person
- *Picking Teams* is funnier, *The Boy without a Name* more serious
- *Picking Teams* is spoken by a child, *The Boy without a Name* by an adult
- *Picking Teams* rhymes alternate lines, *The Boy without a Name* has one rhyme per stanza (more, raw, wore etc.)
- *The Boy without a Name* uses a metaphor (*rusty iron mask*) and harder words (*infinitely, eczema*)
- *The Boy without a Name* uses inference (stanzas 6 and 11)

(Text level 7: *to compare and contrast poems on similar themes, particularly their form and language, discussing personal responses and preferences.*)

Sentence level reading

Ask for a list of adverbs used in *Picking Teams* (*always, usually, first, sometimes, once*) and in *The Boy without a Name* (*clearly, confidently, similarly, never, often*). Sort them into ones to do with time and *–ly* adverbs that tell you *how* something was done. Which poem has most of which sort? Try removing the adverbs from the poems: what difference is made? Then try putting other adverbs in place of those listed: do the poems sound better or worse?
(Sentence level 4: *to identify adverbs and understand their functions in sentences…*)

Word level reading

Make a list of all the words in the poem that have the *or* sound in them. Talk about the different letter strings that make the same sound. Do PCM 13a or the easier version PCM 13b. (Word level 3: *to use independent spelling strategies…*)

PCM 13a

Or words

There are a lot of words containing the *or* sound in *The Boy Without a Name*.
Find the words and write them in the correct box.

or [ ]   **aw** [ ]   **oar** [ ]

augh [ ]   **our** [ ]   **au** [ ]

ore [ ]

The answers to all these clues include the *or* sound.
Solve the clues then check the spelling in a dictionary.

A loud noise sometimes made when asleep   sn_____

To chew with the front teeth   gn_____

A girl who is someone's child   d_____ter

To store away a collection of things   h_____d

Someone travelling about on holiday   t_____ist

Summer month   _____gust

Different tastes of food or drink   flav_____s

Season when the leaves fall off the trees   _____tumn

The most popular   fav_____ite

To move around on hands and knees   cr_____l

Large musical instrument often found in churches   _____gan

If you have time, you can add more words to the boxes, but don't forget to
check the spellings in a dictionary.

PCM 13b

Or words

These words appear in the poem *The Boy Without a Name.*
They all contain the *or* sound.

more	ignore	raw	wore
flaw	swore	ordinary	saw
four	corridor	straw	or

Write them in the correct box.

_or_    **_ore_**    **_aw_**

oar    **_our_**

The answers to all these clues include the *or* sound.
Solve the clues then check the spelling in a dictionary.

The sound made by a lion	r_____
4 lots of 10	f_____ty
A loud noise sometimes made when asleep	sn_____
Open mouth, when tired	y_____n
Food that has not been cooked	r_____
To tip milk out of a jug	p_____

Put a circle round the letters that make the *or* sound.

shore	morning	crawl	core	your
torn	torch	orchard	jaw	fourteen
awful	explore	tour	oars	porch

Add all the words to the correct box at the top of the sheet.

Activities for the Literacy Hour

Only Snow

Year 4, Term 2

Text level reading and writing

Share and enjoy *Only Snow*. Discuss:

- How is the snowfall described in the first stanza?
- How do the children react to the snow? What is their mood?
- How does the teacher react? What is her mood?
- Who is talking in the third and fourth stanzas?
- Who do you think has the right attitude to the snow at the end: the teacher or the children?
- Why does the writer describe it as *the only snow* in the last line?

The poem describes the snow in a very simple and ordinary way, using hardly any adjectives or adverbs, apart from *only,* and no similes. This is to try to give the feelings of the teacher, who isn't at all excited about the snow, as the children are. Ask the class to brainstorm some adjectives, adjectival phrases and similes that the children in the poem might use to describe the snow from their point of view, e.g. papery, lazily floating, ghostly, falling like feathers, settling like icing etc. They could use these in a poem which tries to describe the snowfall so as to convey the children's mood, attitude and emotions instead of the teacher's: *Not Only Snow.* Alternatively, the children could imitate the approach of the poem by writing in a similar way about *Only a Rainbow, Only Thunder and Lightning* or *Only the Wind.* (Text level 4: *to understand how the use of expressive and descriptive language can, e.g. create moods, arouse expectations, build tension, describe attitudes or emotions.* Text level 13: *to write own examples of descriptive, expressive language based on those read. Link to work on adjectives and similes.*)

Sentence level reading and writing

Highlight these words in the poem: *then, though, after all, before, but, while.* Ask the children what job they do in the writing. They are all connectives, a type of word or phrase used to connect different sentences or different parts of a sentence. Investigate what each of these words does in the writing. Those that have a full stop in front of them (*then, after all*) are joining sentences together, those that have a comma or no punctuation in front are joining parts of a sentence together (*though, before, but, while*). Try reading out the poem leaving out these connectives: the writing doesn't flow as well without them. Finally, ask the children to write sentences that use some of these connectives. (Sentence level 4: *to recognise how commas, connectives and full stops are used to join and separate clauses; to identify in their writing where each is more effective.*)

Word level reading

How many words can the children find in the poem that contain the vowel digraph *ea*? *(teacher, teased, earth, weather, really, steamy)* Can they use these words to help them spell other words, e.g. dreamy, leather? Look at PCM 14a or the easier version PCM 14b (Word level 3: *to use independent spelling strategies...*)

PCM 14a

Ea words

The letters *ea* make a different sound in different words.
Put these words into the correct box for *ea* sounds.

leather
reach
early
nearly
heavy
speak
beaten
gear
heard
mean
learn
deaf
dear
leader

*te**ea**cher*	***ea**rth*	*w**ea**ther*	*r**ea**lly*

Can you think of any more *ea* words to put in the boxes?

Make up some sentences using two or more *ea* words in each sentence.
The first has been done for you.

1. I had to <u>speak</u> loudly because the old lady was <u>nearly</u> <u>deaf</u>.

2. _____

3. _____

4. _____

5. _____

PCM 14b

Ea words

The letters *ea* make a different sound in different words
Put these words into the correct box for ea sounds.

*te**a**cher*	*w**ea**ther*

steamy
teased
leather
reach
heavy
speak
beaten
healthy
mean
deaf
leader
spread
bread
head

Can you think of any more *ea* words to put in the boxes?

Complete these sentences with *ea words* from the boxes above.

1. The children were excited because the _____ was sunny.

2. The _____ marked the children's books.

3. The box was too _____ to lift.

4. The jam was _____ thickly on the _____ .

5. I had to _____ loudly because the old lady was nearly _____ .

PCM 14b

Activities for the Literacy Hour
The Mad Professor's Daughter
Year 4, Term 2

Text level reading
Read aloud and enjoy the longer narrative poem *The Mad Professor's Daughter*. Talk about other story poems it reminds the class of, e.g. *The Pied Piper of Hamelin*. Ask them to describe the patterns of rhyme and rhythm in the poem. There are alternate stanzas of six and four lines; the second, fourth and sixth lines always rhyme; the last line of the six-line stanzas is repeated at the start of the four-line one with '*Yes...*' at the front, as a refrain. Prepare a choral reading of *The Mad Professor's Daughter*, emphasising the patterns of rhyme and regular rhythm: the stanzas could be divided up between different groups or individuals. Children could act out the story in mime as it's being read aloud. (Text level 7: *to identify different patterns of rhyme and verse in poetry, e.g. choruses, rhyming couplets, alternate rhyme lines and to read these aloud effectively.*)

Text and sentence level reading
Focus on descriptive and figurative language in the poem. Ask the children to identify descriptive language, any adjectives or adjective phrases used to describe the mad professor's daughter: *quite unsmiling, polite, silent, quiet;* or to describe the weather: *overcast, warm and wild, wet.* Pick out figurative language, any metaphors and similes used to describe her: *as black as night, green as grass, paper-white, red as blood;* or to describe the other children: *like swimmers under water, a wisp of hope rose in our hearts, like sheep we were, like lambs to the slaughter.* How is the setting described to make the story seem more frightening? (e.g. the thunderstorm, the mad face at the window, chains and cobwebs)

Talk about the way that this expressive language makes the poem very dramatic and slightly over the top, creating a scary but enjoyable atmosphere. (Text level 4: *to understand how the use of expressive and descriptive language can, e.g. create moods, arouse expectations, build tension, describe attitudes or emotions;* Text level 5: *to understand the use of figurative language in poetry and prose; compare poetic phrasing with narrative/descriptive examples; locate use of simile.* Sentence level 1: *to revise and extend work on adjectives from Y3 term 2 and link to work on expressive and figurative language in stories and poetry.*)

Text level writing
Get the children to write short descriptions of 'the mad professor's son' based on the type of descriptive and figurative language used in the poem. Brainstorm some expressive adjectives, metaphors and similes which are slightly exaggerated like those in the poem. The writing can be in prose, in unrhyming poetry or, for able children, a stanza in a form similar to Allan Ahlberg's poem. The descriptions can be read (and acted) out in an appropriately melodramatic voice at the end of the lesson! (Text level 13: *to write own examples of descriptive, expressive language based on those read. Link to work on adjectives and similes.*)

Activities for the Literacy Hour

Scabs

Year 4, Term 2

Text level writing

Share aloud and enjoy *Scabs*. Talk about the adjectives used to describe the scabs in each stanza. Ask the children to use the structure of *Scabs* to invent some more stanzas for the poem. They need to insert a new name into line one, a new adjective into line two, which need not be an *–ical* one, and then add two lines of explanation, which can rhyme or not, as preferred, e.g:

The scab on *Amy's* knee
Is *educational*.
Batt School 1993:
Fell over in the playground.

Alternatively, the poem could be changed to reflect a different injury, e.g.

The bump on *Grace's* head
Is *fictional*.
Sitting in the book corner:
Hit by *Harry Potter 4.*

(Text level 13: *to write own examples of descriptive, expressive language based on those read. Link to work on adjectives and similes*)

Word level reading

Focus on the use of adjectives ending in *–ical* in each stanza. Ask for the nouns to which this suffix has been added to make the adjectives, e.g. geography, history, psychology, bibliography, identity, economy. What about *pugilistical* (pugilist?) and *diabolical* (no corresponding noun): ask whether they follow the same pattern. Complete the tables in PCM 15 and then try to use some of the new *–ical* words found to write some more lines for *Scabs*. (Word level 13: *a range of suffixes that can be added to nouns and verbs to make adjectives…*)

Sentence level reading

Focus on the use of possessive apostrophes in the poem. List the examples in the poem: *Jean's knee, Henry's knee,* etc. Talk about how the *–'s* is short for 'belonging to'. Mention that originally in English people used to say 'Henry his knee' until eventually this was shortened to *–'s* for everything, male or female.

Ask for the odd one out in the apostrophes used in the poem: *twins' knees.* Ask why this is different (a common noun, not a proper noun or name; plural not singular). Because plurals end in –*s* already, we don't usually another –*'s* on the end. Talk about the way we make possessives with plural nouns by putting the apostrophe *after* the –*s.* Go through some other examples, e.g. the girls' dresses, the boys' games, the friends' quarrel, etc. Mention plurals that do not end in –*s* (children, men, mice) and so add –*'s* to make possessives.

Discuss the rules for names ending in –*s.* Ask for examples of first names (Jess, Chris, Les) and surnames (Gibbs, Evans, Potts). How do the children think these are usually made into possessives? Children with names like these should be able to answer! It's possible to either put the apostrophe after the final –*s* (Chris' turn) or more usually to add an another –*'s* (Chris's turn). (Sentence level 2: *to use the apostrophe accurately to mark possession…*)

PCM 15

Scabs

1. Complete the table by writing in the missing nouns. Use a dictionary to help with spellings. The first one is done for you:

NOUN	SUFFIX	ADJECTIVE
Geography	–ical	Geographical
	–ical	Historical
	–ical	Psychological
	–ical	Bibliographical
	–ical	Identical
	–ical	Economical

Most nouns drop just the *y* when they add *–ical*. Which noun is the odd one out?

_____

2. Now write in the missing adjectives. Use a dictionary for spellings:

NOUN	SUFFIX	ADJECTIVE
Symmetry	–ical	
Alphabet	–ical	
Geometry	–ical	
Logic	–ical	
Tragic	–ical	

3. If you have time, find some more nouns which change into adjectives by adding *–ical*:

NOUN	SUFFIX	ADJECTIVE
	–ical	
	–ical	
	–ical	

Activities for the Literacy Hour

Teacher's Prayer

Year 4, Term 3

Text level reading

Read aloud and enjoy *Teacher's Prayer*. Talk about how the poem is written in a regular rhythm and rhyme scheme. Count aloud the seven syllables in each line (except lines 11 and 14) and clap out the rhythm of four stressed and three unstressed syllables in these regular lines (*LET the CHILdren IN our CARE*). Ask the children to identify the pattern of the rhymes and explain how rhyming is usually described, using letters to stand for each rhyme word, i.e. in this poem AA,BB,CC,DD in each of the two stanzas, or groups of lines. Mention that pairs of lines which rhyme like this are usually called rhyming couplets. Finish with a class performance of the poem which brings out the regular rhyme and rhythm, as discussed.

Stress that the poem is supposed to be a prayer and ask the children to chant it in an appropriate way. The lines beginning *Let...*could be read by an individual or group narrator and the other lines divided up between different individuals, pairs or groups of children to achieve a choral effect. (Text level 4: *understand the following terms and identify them in poems: verse, chorus, couplet, stanza, rhyme, rhythm, alliteration;* Text level 5: *to clap out and count the syllables in each line of regular poetry;* Text level 6: *to describe how a poet does or does not use rhyme...*)

Sentence level reading

Ask the class to focus on the order of the words in each sentence in the poem. How does each sentence begin? (*Let the children* or *Let them*). Why do all the sentences begin with a verb like this? What type of sentence is this? Discuss how this word order is used in commands, when we want someone to do something for us (e.g. *Pass* the salt. *Let* us pray. *Do* your work). A prayer is a special sort of command sentence because it is requesting or asking for something rather than demanding it. Experiment with changing the command sentences into statements, i.e.:

The children in our care
Clean their shoes and comb their hair;
They come to school on time – and neat,
Blow their noses, wipe their feet.
They do not eat in class
Or rush into the hall *en masse*. Etc.

Talk about what has to be changed in the order of the words and what stays the same. (Sentence level 3: *to understand how the grammar of a sentence alters when the sentence type is altered...*)

Text level writing

Tell the class they are going to write a 'Pupil's Prayer', using *Teacher's Prayer* as their model. Read or perform the poem again and discuss the kind of things the teacher prays for, the qualities he would like his pupils to have and not to have. Point out that stanza one is mostly about positive features and stanza two about negative ones. Brainstorm the things which pupils might pray for. What kind of qualities in their teacher(s) would they ask for and which ones would they not like their teacher(s) to have? List these on the board. Ask the group to follow the model of *Teacher's Prayer* for the structure of their poem. This means using rhyming couplets and a seven-syllable line with four beats in each, as discussed in the whole-class session about the poem. PCM 16 gives a writing frame adapted from *Teacher's Prayer* which children could use for their own poems, if appropriate. Other ideas children could explore might be:

- The caretaker's prayer
- The headteacher's prayer
- The dinner lady's prayer
- The school secretary's prayer
- The P.E. teacher's prayer
- The school nurse's prayer

(Text level 14: *to write poems, experimenting with different styles and structures, discuss if and why different forms are more suitable than others.*)

PCM 16

Pupil's prayer

Write your own version of Allan Ahlberg's poem by filling in the lines below.
Follow the pattern of rhymes shown at the side.
A rhyming dictionary will help you to find rhyme words.

Stanza One	**Rhymes**
Let the teachers in our school	A
_____	A
Come to school on time and neat	B
_____	B

Stanza Two	**Rhymes**
Let them, Lord, **not** _____	C
_____	C
Let them _____	D
Let them _____	D

Activities for the Literacy Hour

Lost

Year 4, Term 3

Text level writing

Read and enjoy *Lost*. Talk about funny notes that parents sometimes send from home (quote examples!) and things that children lose in school. Invite children to share their own experiences of these things.

Look at how the poem is written. Why do some of the lines have a full stop or semi-colon in the middle of them? How does this sound when the poem is read aloud? Discuss how the poem is written to sound rather jerky and rambling like a real letter someone has written quickly before school starts.

Ask whether it rhymes and get the children to describe the structure of pairs of rhyming couplets in each stanza. Talk about how the poem mixes smooth rhyming with jerky breaks in the lines. Children can then write an example of a letter to Mrs Butler themselves complaining about something lost: these could be in prose or verse but need not follow the same structure as the poem. PCM 17 provides a simple letter framework. (Text level 4: *understand the following terms and identify them in poems: verse, chorus, couplet, stanza, rhyme, rhythm, alliteration;* Text level 6: *to describe how a poet does or does not use rhyme…*)

Sentence level reading:

Ask the children to pick out all the different kinds of punctuation marks in *Lost*: commas, full stops, semi-colon, dash, question mark and brackets. Highlight these on an enlarged version of the text and discuss how they affect the way we read the poem. Then read the poem aloud as a whole class trying to reflect the punctuation in the pattern of pauses and intonation used.

More able children could set the poem out in the style of a real letter and compare their punctuation to that of the original. How does the use of capital letters have to change? (Sentence level 2: *to identify the common punctuation marks including commas, semi-colons, colons, dashes, hyphens, speech marks, and to respond to them appropriately when reading.*)

Word level reading:

Pick out the lines: *she knitted it and it's pure wool.* Ask the children what *it's* stands for here. Does it mean 'belonging to it' or 'it is'? Try out both meanings in the sentence to show that only the second one can fit here. Remind the children that *its* meaning 'belonging to it' *never* has an apostrophe, so if they see *it's,* with an apostrophe, it *always* stands for 'it is' or sometimes 'it has'. Ask for another example in the poem of *it's* meaning 'it is' (*it's purplish and green*). PCM 18 can be used for further reinforcement of the difference between *its* and *it's.* (Word level 10: *to distinguish the two forms: its (possessive no apostrophe) and it's (contracted 'it is') and to use these accurately in own writing.*)

PCM 17

Dear Mrs Butler

_____

_____

_____

_____

Dear Mrs Butler,

This is just a note about …

Best wishes,

Yours sincerely,

_____(Mrs)

P.S.

Dear Mrs Butler

PCM 18

Is it *its* or is it *it's*?

REMEMBER!

It's always means 'it is' or 'it has'. For example: *It's easy-peasy! It's been easy-peasy!*

Its always means 'belonging to it'. For example: *The dog found its bone. The horse lost its shoe.*

Put either *its* or *it's* into the spaces in these sentences:

1. _____ pure wool.

2. _____ purplish and green.

3. The cat lost _____ whiskers.

4. The coat was on_____ peg.

5. _____ just a note about our Raymond's coat.

6. The swimming towel was not in _____ right place.

7. _____ in the pocket of his coat.

8. The hat is old and _____ his father's.

9. The coat had the note in _____ pocket.

10. The sock had a darn in _____ heel.

Imagine your mum is writing a letter to your teacher about something you've lost at school. Write some more sentences that use *it's* and *its* correctly.

Dear Mr/Mrs _____ ,

    This is just a note about

Activities for the Literacy Hour
Sale of Work
Year 4, Term 3

Text level reading and writing
Perform *Sale of Work* with the class: it should be read aloud in the voice of an auctioneer or market trader. Talk about the form of the poem: a free verse structure which does not use rhyme. Tell the class they are going to write their own *Sale of Work* poem about things in the classroom. Ask the children to look around the room and pick out things which could be included in the sale. Tell them to look carefully and not to suggest the first thing they see. Then give the children time to share ideas in pairs, before asking the whole class for suggestions for the poem. Use the framework given on PCM 19 to draft a whole-class poem on the board or large sheet of paper using the children's suggestions. Individual poems can also be written during the independent group time using copies of PCM 19 or asking pupils to devise their own similar free verse structures, as appropriate to their ability. (Text level 14: *to write poems, experimenting with different styles and structures, discuss if and why different forms are more suitable than others.*)

Sentence level reading
Ask the children how many different punctuation marks they can find in *Sale of Work,* i.e. colons, commas, full stops, question marks, exclamation marks and a dash. Talk about the function of the colons in the poem (to introduce lists) and the dash (to indicate an afterthought). Ask how we change our voice in reading aloud when a line ends with a colon, dash, question mark or exclamation mark. Ask the children to read aloud the poem as a whole class, taking into account the punctuation marks as discussed. In writing their own versions of *Sale of Work*, the children can also use the range of punctuation marks identified. (Sentence level 2: *to identify the common punctuation marks including commas, semi-colons, colons, dashes, hyphens, speech marks, and to respond to them appropriately when reading.*)

Word level:
Focus on these words in the poem: *handwriting, newsbook, brand-new.* Ask what they have in common. If the children can't guess, give some more examples of compound words (e.g. playground, classroom, handmade). Brainstorm other examples of compound words like these. Children can then investigate which ones are printed as single words in the dictionary, which ones are hyphenated and which are still two words. A quick way to find out is to type the words in to a word-processing program with a spell-checker! Children can also explore which of the compound words they've listed are nouns like *handwriting* and which are adjectives like *brand-new.* Can they find any verbs which are compound words (e.g. to brainstorm, to nit-pick, to blacklist)? (Word level 11: *to investigate compound words and recognise that they can aid spelling even where pronunciation obscures it...*)

PCM 19
Sale of work

Who wants to buy

_____

_____

_____

_____

Price reduced for quick sale

_____

_____

Delivery can be arranged.

What am I bid

_____

_____

Hurry, hurry, hurry

_____ going cheap

_____

Activities for the Literacy Hour

Mrs So-and-So

Year 4, Term 3

Text level reading

Read aloud and enjoy *Mrs So-and-So*, emphasising the rhythm of a playground skipping song. Talk about stand-in teachers and the problems they face, and compare *Supply Teacher* (*PMB* 16-17*).* Get the whole class to clap and count out the syllables in each line (a pattern of 4,4, 7,4,4,7 in each stanza). Ask for (pre-selected?) volunteers to actually skip out the rhythm while a stanza of the poem is being chanted. Do the children know any other skipping songs which follow the same rhythm? These could be performed as well.

Talk about why the rhythm of the poem is suitable for skipping to. Why would it be harder if there were more beats in each line? Ask the children to identify and describe the rhyme scheme in the poem (ABCDEC). Do other skipping songs rhyme like this, with the two long lines rhyming and the same rhyme used throughout? (Text level 5: *to clap out and count the syllables in each line of regular poetry;* Text level 6: *to describe how a poet does or does not use rhyme...;* Text level 7: *to recognise some simple forms of poetry and their uses, e.g. the regularity of skipping songs...*)

Sentence level reading

Ask the children to identify the punctuation marks used in the poem: commas, full stops, dashes, exclamation marks, question marks, ellipsis (...). Discuss how these affect a reading aloud of the poem, especially the last three in the list. Make notes on an enlarged copy of the poem and practise varying intonation and using pauses in reading to reflect the patterns of punctuation. (Sentence level 2: *to identify the common punctuation marks including commas, semi-colons, colons, dashes, hyphens, speech marks, and to respond to them appropriately when reading.*)

Word level reading

Focus on the rhyming words: *know, snow, row, go, so-and-so.* Brainstorm other rhyming words which have the same long vowel phoneme *'oa'* and divide them into groups according to the spelling pattern they follow, e.g.

bow, show, elbow, flow, below, etc.
hoe, doe, foe, Joe, toe, woe, etc.
ago, cello, demo, hello, no, fro, etc.
though, although, etc.

List other words with the same spelling patterns but different sounds:

now, to, do, through, tough, bough etc.

Read the poem *Hints on Pronunciation for Foreigners* on PCM 20 and discuss spelling patterns and their exceptions further in a humorous context! (Word level 3: *to use independent spelling strategies...*)

PCM 20

Hints on pronunciation for foreigners

Read the poem slowly! The rhymes will help you with how to say some of the words.
Circle any words you don't know how to say and ask an adult or look in a dictionary for some help.

I take it you already know
Of tough and bough and cough and dough?
Others may stumble, but not you
On hiccough, thorough, laugh, and through.
I write in case you wish perhaps
To learn of less familiar traps.
Beware of heard, a dreadful word
That looks like beard, and sounds like bird.
And dead: it's said like bed, not bead;
For goodness' sake, don't call it 'deed'!
Watch out for meat and great and threat
(They rhyme with suite and straight and debt).
A moth is not a moth in mother,
Nor both in bother, broth in brother.
And here is not a match for there,
Nor dear for bear, or fear for pear.
There's dose and rose, there's also lose
(Just look them up), and goose and choose,
And cork and work, and card and ward,
And font and front, and word and sword,
And do and go and thwart and cart –
Come, come! I've barely made a start!
A dreadful language? Man alive,
I'd mastered it when I was five!

(Anonymous)

Activities for the Literacy Hour

There's a Fish Tank
Year 4, Term 3

Text level reading and writing:

Read *There's a Fish Tank*. Ask the children to list all the missing things mentioned in the poem. How many are in their own classroom? Can they look round their own classroom and mention any other unfinished things that could be added to the poem? Talk about how the poem works by repeating a similar phrase structure using 'without' or 'with no'. Tell the group they are going to write their own collaborative poem about unfinished things by using just these phrase structures and nothing else. It will be what's called a list poem, since it will look like a long list on the page. Ask the group to brainstorm other examples of incomplete things, but not only in the classroom, e.g. a foot without a shoe, a pen without ink, a peg without a coat, etc. When they have come up with a number of these, encourage the group to think of some other examples that might rhyme with the ones collected so far, e.g. a snooker player with no cue, a chain with no link, a river without a boat, etc. As a whole group or in pairs, the children can then draft out their own 'Missing Things' poem by simply listing the objects, either in free verse or in rhyming pairs:

a foot without a shoe,
a snooker player with no cue
a pen without ink
a chain with no link, etc.

Finally, encourage the children to think of an effective way of ending the list poem, e.g. a poem that's come to an end, a poem without an end, or a brain that can't think of any more! (Text level 14: *to write poems, experimenting with different styles and structures, discuss if and why different forms are more suitable than others.*)

Sentence level reading:

Give the children a copy of PCM 21, which is the poem with all punctuation marks (14) deleted. Ask them to put in, wherever they feel is appropriate:

● full stops
● commas
● semi-colons

Give them the original version of the poem, so that they can compare their punctuation with that used by Allan Ahlberg. Talk about any differences. Focus on the use of semi-colons to separate items in a list where each item is a phrase or a clause, as in the first stanza of the poem. Remember that alternative punctuation *is* possible in places! (Sentence level 2: *to identify the common punctuation marks, including commas and semi-colons ... and to respond to them appropriately when reading.*)

Word level reading

Look for compound words in the poem (guinea-pig, cupboard, flowerpot, without, waste-paper, etc.) Ask the children to look around their classroom for more examples of compound words (blackboard, bookshelf, homework, noticeboard, doorknob etc.) Reinforce the concept of compound words with PCM 22. (Word level 11: *to investigate compound words and recognise that they can aid spelling even where pronunciation obscures it, e.g. handbag, cupboard*)

Talk about how we can use prefixes and suffixes to show that something is missing (without a friend could be written friend*less*, no hope is hope*less*, *un*finished or *in*complete projects). Complete PCM 23. (Word level 8 : *revise and reinforce earlier work on prefixes and suffixes...*)

PCM 21

There's a poem with no punctuation in it!

All the punctuation marks have been lost from the poem.
Put some punctuation marks back into it.

There's a fish tank
In our class
With no fish in it
A guinea-pig cage
With no guinea-pig in it
A formicarium
With no ants in it
And according to Miss Hodge
Some of our heads
Are empty too

There's a stock-cupboard
With no stock
Flowerpots without flowers
Plimsolls without owners
And me without a friend
For a week
While he goes on holiday

There's a girl
With no front teeth
And a boy with hardly any hair
Having had it cut
There are sums without answers
Paintings unfinished
And projects with no hope
Of ever coming to an end
According to Miss Hodge
The only thing that's brim-full
In our class
Is the waste-paper basket

When you've finished, compare your punctuation to Allan Ahlberg's.
What are the differences?

PCM 22
Compound words

Change these words into compound words by adding a word from the box.

ground	taker	stand	ball
shine	lace		bag
room	board	pole	way
light	hole		case
mark	man	lid	wreck

care_____   play_____   sun_____

moon_____   under_____   cloak_____

key_____   flag_____   eye_____

fire_____   foot_____   ship_____

shoe_____   card_____   rail_____

hand_____   suit_____   book_____

How many compound words can you make beginning with these words?

over *coat*_____   some *thing*_____   out *doors*_____

over_____   some_____   out_____

over_____   some_____   out_____

over_____   some_____   out_____

PCM 23
Prefixes and suffixes

1. In the poem *There's a fish tank* a lot of things are missing.
Change these words to show that something is missing by adding the prefix
un–, the prefix *in–* or the suffix *–less.*

finished   _____ *unfinished* _____

tidy   _____

complete   _____

home   _____

correct   _____

welcome   _____

secure   _____

use   _____

visible   _____

kind   _____

care   _____

power   _____

When you have finished, check your answers in a dictionary.

2. The suffix *–ful* is often added to a word to show that something is present.
Which of the above words can have the suffix *–ful*? The first one is done for
you.

useful_____   _____ful   _____ful

3. Make a list of other words that end with *–ful*.

_____

_____

_____

_____

_____

_____

Part 3:
Activities outside the Literacy Hour

Heard it in the Playground (HP 93-105)
Investigating playground games and language

Session 1
Begin with a reading of the long title poem *Heard it in the Playground.* Talk about the way the poem is written, like a playground chant. Discuss and illustrate features such as:

● repetition
● building up phrases and clauses
● different size fonts to show louder and softer
● skipping rhythms
● expressions children use
● insults
● words that imitate rhythms (*bum-shicka*)
● references to other playground rhymes and games
● references to TV programmes
● slang words (*quality, ace, neat, brill, skill, wicked,* etc.)

Read and discuss other poems about the playground from the two collections, such as *Bags I* (*HP* 30-31), *The Boy Without a Name* (*HP* 44-45) and *Complaint* (*PMB* 32-33).

Session 2
Talk about how the poem could be performed bearing in mind all the above points. Discuss playground language used in the poem and how it differs from standard English. Because playground language is very informal, it uses many slang words and expressions not used in more formal language. Different local words (dialect words) are also sometimes used in different schools. Playground language also has different rhythms from speech used inside school because it is used for games, dips, skipping rhymes and chants. Children can explore the slang words in the poem further using PCM 24.

Divide the class into five or six groups and share out large sections of the poem for them to perform. Give them photocopies of their sections and ask them first to annotate their copies with suggestions for how to read aloud and act out the lines. The children could use a narrator and mime the actions, divide up the lines between several speakers who perform the actions, or a mixture of these approaches. The groups can then perform their sections in sequence and the whole class can evaluate and modify the performances. Audio – or videotaping, if practical – will help this process of reviewing. In the final performance, in a large space if possible, the 'set' of a playground could be made, or, weather permitting, the actual school playground could be used for an open-air performance.

Session 3

Tell the children you want them to investigate playground games and language further. Divide the class into five large groups to research one of these aspects of the topic:

- playground games
- playground skipping rhymes
- playground choosing dips
- playground slang
- other playground activities (e.g. swapping cards)

Initially, the groups will need to brainstorm ideas and existing knowledge in the chosen areas. They then need to come up with research questions they want to try to answer. Filling in the first two columns of a KWL grid, as shown below, will help with this stage:

Playground games

What do I know? (K)	What do I want to find out? (W)	What have I learned? (L)
British bulldog	do other schools play it?	
40-40	what are the rules?	
Football	what do girls think about it?	

Further sessions

The groups will next need to plan how to research their chosen areas. Guide them into approaches such as:

- observing playtimes
- interviewing other children, teachers, parents and grandparents
- corresponding with other schools, possibly in other countries, through email
- carrying out structured surveys
- designing written questionnaires
- looking for information in books, CD-ROMs and the Internet
- using ICT for storing and presenting data

The presentation of the groups' findings could take the form of:

- A rule-book for playground games in the school
- A book of playground games in other local schools
- A book of playground games in other countries or areas
- A book of playground games from other times
- A collection of playground rhymes and dips on tape
- A dictionary of playground slang
- A guide to trading cards

Useful teacher resources are Iona and Peter Opie's *The Lore and Language of Schoolchildren* and *Children's Games in Street and Playground*.

Extension

Following the work on playground games and after reading or re-reading *Complaint* (*PMB* 32-33), the children could investigate what playtime is really like for pupils at school. The children could devise some simple questions to use when interviewing children about playtime, e.g.:

● What do you enjoy about playtime?
● What changes would you like?
● Are our rules for playtime fair?

When the questions have been decided, the children can find other children to interview. The interviews can be recorded on cassette recorders so that all the children can listen to the responses.

● Do the youngest children and the oldest children respond differently?
● Are the older children aware of younger children's anxieties?
● Do all children play in the same area? Or like the same games?
● Are there sufficient things to do at playtime?

As the children reflect on their findings, they may have suggestions for improvements. These could be written in a letter to the headteacher. The children will need to consider an appropriate mood for their letter: polite and respectful letters are more likely to be treated sympathetically than a long list of ill-considered demands. The headteacher will hopefully consider the issues and write an appropriate response. This may not, of course, always be positive. A request for longer playtimes might meet with the response that the Government requires that all children are in lessons for a certain amount of time each day. However, there may be issues that haven't been seen from the point of view of the children and small adjustments to the routine may be made.

This exercise gives the children the opportunity to consider the needs of others and to take an active role in shaping how the school is run.

PCM 24

Heard it in the playground

Here are some slang words used in the poem.
First, say what you think they mean in playground slang.
Then, look them up in a dictionary to find their meanings in standard English.

Word	Slang Meanings	Dictionary Meanings
quality		
skill		
ace		
nice		
neat		
mega		
brill		
wicked		

Which of these expressions is the strongest? Put them in what you think is the best order by writing numbers 1-6 underneath (1 = strongest)

acely-neat   fabby-dabby-dooby   mega-dabby-dooby

_____   _____   _____

dooby-dooby-dooby   acely-dooby   acely-quality

_____   _____   _____

Write some more playground slang words here and give their meanings. You could use them to make a dictionary of playground slang in your school:

_____

_____

Supply Teacher and *Blame* (*PMB* pp16-17 & 22)
Personal and social education

Read aloud and enjoy the two poems. They are both very funny poems but they are about situations which we have all been in at school or at home. Ask the class what theme the two poems have in common, i.e. they are both about blaming other people for what we do, either blaming another teacher or another child. Give the children a few minutes to think of times when they have done similar things to those described in the poem and ask them to share these initially in pairs. Listen to some examples of these experiences as a whole class. Ask the children to role-play in groups of four the situation in *Blame*: they should improvise the situation rather than read out the words of the poem. Tell the children in the role of teacher that they have to decide what action to take, who's to blame and what to say to the boys in the poem. After the groups have done this, share some of the 'teacher's' responses with the whole class and ask the 'pupils' in the same groups what they thought of the 'teacher's' actions and words.

Small Quarrel & *It is a Puzzle* (*PMB* pp26-27 & 48-49)
Personal and social education

Read aloud and enjoy the two poems. Talk about the relationships between the girls in each poem. Why do they behave in the way they do? Why do such small things become so important in situations like *Small Quarrel*? Why do people pretend like the girl in *It is a Puzzle*? Do boys behave in the same way or is this sort of behaviour special to girls' friendships? Ask the children to think of experiences they have had with friendships which are like the ones described in the poems. How did they behave and what happened? Let the children share these in pairs initially and then listen to some as a whole class. It will be important to be sensitive to anything which is likely to upset or offend any of the children in the group and the class need to be aware of this in their discussions. Ask the children to role-play in fours the situations in either of the poems, improvising what they say and do. Ask for feedback at the end on what it felt like to be in the situation and the role being played.

A *Please Mrs Butler* day

Organise a day when children and staff in a particular class or year dress up as characters from the *Mrs Butler* books. Presentations by teachers and pupils can be made of favourite performance poems from the two books, for example:

- *Scissors* (*PMB* 56-57)
- *Colin* (*PMB* 64-65)
- *Why Must we Go to School?*(*HP* 21)
- *Not now, Nigel* (*HP* 25-26)
- *Parents' Evening* (*HP* 36-37)

The Trial of Derek Drew (*HP* 47–49) can be presented in appropriate costume as a piece of courtroom drama.

Schooling (HP 81-91) can be presented as a series of short pieces or sketches by individuals and groups.

Children can write in role some of the following:

- a school report by Mrs Butler or Miss Hodge for one of the children in the poems, e.g. Graham Prewitt, Derek Drew, Glenis Parker, Billy McBone etc.
- an advert for a new teacher to work at the school
- a register of all the children and a list of the teachers mentioned in the poems
- Emma Hackett's newsbook or newsbooks by other children
- Mrs Butler's diary
- a name, uniform and motto/logo for the school
- some entries for a school log book
- an Inspector's report on the school

The day can also include children singing songs from *Heard it in the Playground* for which tunes are suggested, such as:

- *The Grumpy Teacher* ('The Drunken Sailor')
- *The Mrs Butler Blues* (any blues tune!)
- *Leavers' Song* ('Goodbye Old Paint' from the film *Shane*, and also Aaron Copland's *Billy the Kid*)
- *The Bell* ('Me and My Gal')

The Mrs Butler Songbook by Allan Ahlberg and Colin Matthews (Viking 1992) provides music and performance ideas for all of the above except *The Bell*, and also some 32 other poems from the two *Mrs Butler* books. There is also a Puffin Audio Cassette of *Please Mrs Butler Poems and Songs*.

The day could end with a performance of the poem *Heard it in the Playground* by a large cast: 'a whole classful of children belting it out' as Allan Ahlberg imagines it!

Poetry anthologies

The children can compile individual, group or class anthologies of school poems by other poets. They could use some of the headings from the two *Mrs Butler* books to organise the poems selected ('School Time', 'Play Time', 'Dinner Time', 'Home Time', or alternatively 'Short Ones', 'Long Ones') or make up their own form of organisation. Children can include their own poems inspired by the *Mrs Butler* books in the anthologies. Useful books to use to find poems on all aspects of school life would be:

- *Excuses, Excuses,* ed. John Foster (Oxford University Press 1997)
- *School's Out!* ed. John Foster (Oxford University Press 1988)
- *The Secret Lives of Teachers,* ed. Brian Moses (Macmillan 1996)
- *Poems about School,* ed. Brian Moses (Wayland 1999)
- *Nine O'Clock Bell,* ed. Raymond Wilson (Puffin 1985)

The finished anthologies could be added to the class or school library or shared with children in other schools, possibly via the Internet.

About Allan Ahlberg

PCM 25 has information about Allan Ahlberg's life and books in note form which children could use to write paragraphs about the author. This could be as part of a book week activity, as background to the Mrs Butler poems, as an author study or as a piece of non-fiction, biographical writing.

PCM 25

About Allan Ahlberg

Use these notes to write some paragraphs about Allan Ahlberg's life and books:

Born 1938 in London.

Worked, lot of different jobs: postman, gravedigger, soldier, plumber's mate.

Trained to be teacher, Sunderland College of Education.

Met wife, Janet, at college. She training to be primary school teacher too.

Taught ten years in primary school.

First book called *Brick Street Boys* published 1975. Wrote it so his wife had a story to illustrate.

Janet and Allan Ahlberg became famous partnership. Stopped teaching to work full-time on children's books.

Allan wrote words, Janet drew pictures for many well-known children's picture books, e.g *Burglar Bill* (1977), *Cops and Robbers* (1978), *Each Peach Pear Plum* (1978), *Happy Families* (1980), *Peepo* (1981), *The Jolly Postman* (1986) etc.

They published novels for older readers, e.g. *It Was a Dark and Stormy Night* (1993), joke books like *The Ha Ha Bonk Book* (1982).

Please Mrs Butler published 1983 and *Heard it in the Playground* in 1989. Both illustrated by Fritz Wegner.

Heard it in the Playground won the Signal Award for children's poetry in 1990.

Other poetry books: *The Mighty Slide* (1988), illustrated by Charlotte Voake and *The Mysteries of Zigomar* (1997), illustrated by John Lawrence.

Allan and Janet had a daughter called Jessica.

Janet Ahlberg died in 1994.

Allan Ahlberg lives just outside Leicester in England.

Also available from Questions...

QUESTIONS LITERACY RESOURCES

Every teacher is aware of the importance of capturing children's interest when teaching reading. Based on the hugely popular story characters that are familiar to almost every primary school child, these packs have been prepared to support Literacy Hour sessions with individual and group follow-up tasks.

Photocopiable pages are provided with activities suitable for text, sentence and word-level work, which children will love doing. All of the ideas have been devised, tried and tested by teachers, and are differentiated to meet the needs of all readers in the class.

Story of Tracy Beaker – Literacy Resource Pack
Compiled by Elizabeth Ross-Elsden

Featuring the character of Tracy Beaker, from Jacqueline Wilson's award-winning tale, children read extracts from the story and complete tasks that develop their reading skills and extend their comprehension of the text. There are also creative writing activities designed to appeal to reluctant writers and plenty of topic ideas to link the story to other curriculum areas.

ISBN: 1-898149-82-8
Price: £14.99

Bill's New Frock – Literacy Resource Pack
Compiled by Marian Dean

Following a day in the life of the character Bill Simpson from Anne Fine's story, this pack is designed to capitalise on children's enthusiasm to read about his adventures by providing a range of ideas and photocopiable worksheets. Through studying text extracts children are encouraged to develop a sense of the book as a whole, with some activities promoting further reading beyond the Literacy Hour period.

ISBN: 1-84190-030-3
Price: £14.99

If you would like to place an order for these publications or would like to receive more information on the full range of products available from Questions Publishing Limited you can phone us on 0121 212 0919 or fax us on 0121 212 0959 or write to us at: The Questions Publishing Company Limited, Customer Services, 27 Frederick Street, Birmingham B1 3HH.

Also available from Questions...

Flying High With Literacy 1
Joy McCormick and Narinderjit Gill

This practical book explores a range of techniques and strategies to enhance learning in literacy. This book shows you how you can build on existing teaching skills to link with the National Literacy Strategy. The book explores a range of techniques and strategies to enhance teaching and learning in literacy, helping teachers to think about their own practice. Chapters cover:

- choosing a teaching style
- using questions to develop learning
- helping children to access research
- the modelling process
- developing group work
- building literacy skills using the school library.

ISBN: 1-84190-017-6
Price: £12.99

Flying High With Literacy 2
Joy McCormick and Narinderjit Gill

Working with non-fiction is a key part of the National Literacy Strategy, but one major problem is in finding suitable texts to work with. This book provides specially written texts and source material for a range of purposes. Each section provides a framework for studying a piece of text, examples of class or group activities, a framework for children for writing their own text and ideas for follow-up activities. With these examples of letter writing, report writing, persuasive writing, discussion writing and procedural writing, you need never write your own literacy materials again!

ISBN: 1-84190-018-4
Price: £12.99

If you would like to place an order for these publications or would like to receive more information on the full range of products available from Questions Publishing Limited you can phone us on 0121 212 0919 or fax us on 0121 212 0959 or write to us at: The Questions Publishing Company Limited, Customer Services, 27 Frederick Street, Birmingham B1 3HH.

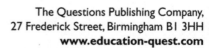

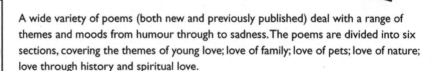